A TRUE BOOK™

W9-AMN-118

The
Moon

ELAINE LANDAU

Children's Press®
A Division of Scholastic Inc.
New York   Toronto   London   Auckland   Sydney
Mexico City   New Delhi   Hong Kong
Danbury, Connecticut

Content Consultant

Michelle Yehling

Astronomy Education Consultant

Aurora, Illinois

Reading Consultant

Linda Cornwell

Literacy Consultant

Carmel, Indiana

Library of Congress Cataloging-in-Publication Data

Landau, Elaine.
The Moon / by Elaine Landau.
    p. cm.—(A true book)
Includes bibliographical references and index.
ISBN-13: 978-0-531-12562-5 (lib. bdg.)   978-0-531-14792-4 (pbk.)
ISBN-10: 0-531-12562-9 (lib. bdg.)   0-531-14792-4 (pbk.)
1. Moon—Juvenile literature. I. Title. II. Series.
QB582.L353 2008
523.3—dc22   2007004183

All rights reserved. Published in 2008 by Children's Press, an imprint of Scholastic Inc.
Published simultaneously in Canada. Printed in the United States of America.
SCHOLASTIC, CHILDREN'S PRESS, A TRUE BOOK, and associated logos are trademarks and/or registered trademarks of Scholastic Inc.
1 2 3 4 5 6 7 8 9 10 R 17 16 15 14 13 12 11 10 09

DISCARD

Find the Truth!

Everything you are about to read is true *except* for one of the sentences on this page.

Which one is **TRUE**?

T or F   There are footprints on the moon right now.

T or F   Noises sound louder on the moon than they do on Earth.

Find the answer in this book.

Contents

THE BIG TRUTH!

A person who weighs 100 pounds on Earth would weigh 17 pounds on the moon.

4 Moonscape

How was the moon formed?

5 Going to the Moon

Could you live on the moon?
Would you want to?

Astronauts and their equipment left footprints and tire tracks on the moon.

Here you see the full moon over an Arizona desert.

CHAPTER 1

Meet the Moon

The moon appears bigger when it is low in the sky.

Look up at the sky tonight. You may see many stars. Yet one object will stand out above all the others. It is the moon. The moon is the brightest object in the night sky. People have been gazing at the moon for thousands of years. They have been trying to understand Earth's closest neighbor in space.

There are many old stories about and drawings of the moon. People used these to try to understand the moon and all its changes.

Why are people so interested in the moon? One reason is that the moon is the easiest space object to see from Earth. It looks much larger than the stars. The moon is only about 238,855 miles (384,400 kilometers) away from Earth. That is the same distance as traveling around Earth's **equator** almost 10 times. That may seem very far. But when it comes to space travel, it is not. Traveling to the sun would be the same distance as circling Earth's equator almost 4,000 times!

Some cave drawings of the moon are more than 30,000 years old!

An ancient drawing of the moon decorates this cave in France.

Moon

9

Earth's moon is about one-fourth the size of Earth. The distance across the center of the moon is 2,159 miles (3,475 km). This is about the distance from Chicago to San Francisco.

The moon **orbits**, or travels around, Earth. As the moon orbits, it also **rotates**, or spins. Imagine a slowly spinning top.

Earth's moon is the only one you can easily see. But it is not the only moon in the **solar system**. Earth's solar system includes the sun and eight planets. It also includes more than 162 moons! Any large object that orbits a planet is called a moon. Turn the page to see how Earth's moon fits into the solar system.

Saturn has at least 56 moons and Jupiter has 63!

This illustration shows Saturn and five of its moons. The moon that looks the largest here is called Dione.

The Solar System

Pluto (dwarf planet)

Uranus

Jupiter

Mars

Mercury

asteroid belt

The Moon

- Distance from Earth: About 238,855 mi. (384,400 km)
- Diameter: 2,159 mi. (3,475 km)
- Length of orbit around Earth: 29.5 days
- Age: About 4.4 billion years

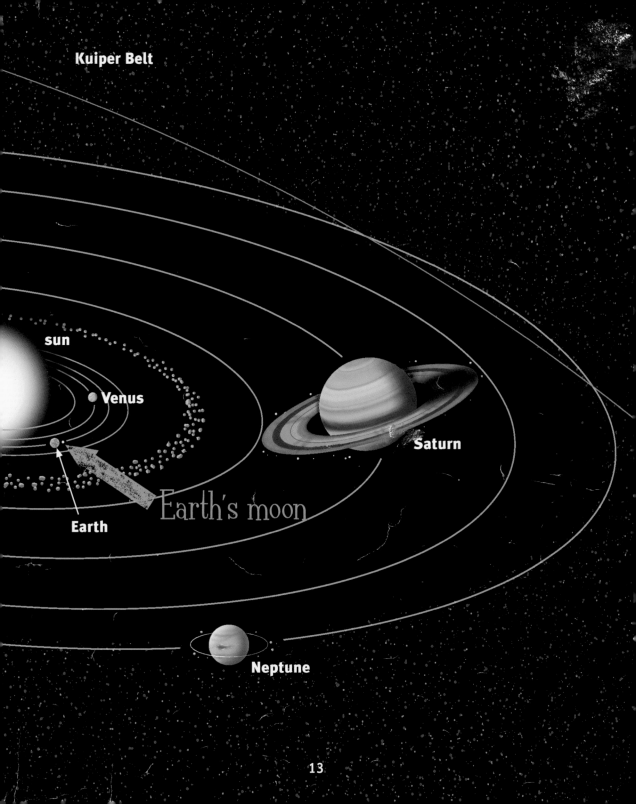

Kuiper Belt

sun

Venus

Saturn

Earth's moon

Earth

Neptune

13

As the moon zooms through space, what keeps it close to Earth? The answer is **gravity**.

Gravity is a force that pulls objects together. As the moon orbits, Earth's gravity pulls on it. This pull keeps the moon from floating out into space.

The moon has less **mass** than Earth. Mass is the amount of matter, or stuff, in an object. Having less mass means having lower gravity. If you were on the moon, you could jump very high. You would feel very light. In fact, you would actually weigh less!

The moon has enough gravity to pull on Earth, however. It tugs at Earth's oceans. That causes water to rise at times. This high water is called a high tide.

High Tide

Low Tide

The moon's pull on Earth's oceans causes high tides.
As Earth turns away from the moon, the pull gets weaker.
This causes low tides.

At twilight, you may be able to see the crescent moon. The crescent is lit up by the sun. The rest of the moon is lit by sunlight that bounces off Earth and hits the moon.

CHAPTER 2

Phases of the Moon

 When the moon looks like a sliver, it's called a crescent moon.

The moon shines brightly in the sky. But its light is not its own. Instead the moon reflects, or bounces back, light from the sun. The moonlight you see is sunlight bouncing off the moon's surface. In Earth's sky, the moon appears to change shape based on how much sunlight is hitting it. These shapes are called **phases**.

The moon never actually changes its shape. Why does it seem to change?

Sunlight lights up half of the moon at any time. This bright half is the only part we can see. As the moon orbits, we see more or less of the bright half from Earth. Use the diagram at right to see the moon's position during a full moon.

The moon completes one orbit of Earth every 29.5 days. At the start of each orbit, the moon is not visible in the sky. This is called a new moon. The period from new moon to new moon is called a lunar month.

When the moon seems to get bigger each night, it is said to be waxing.

What Makes the Moon Full?

moon

Sunlight always falls on half of the moon. As the moon orbits Earth, we see different amounts of the lit half. When we can see all of the moon's lit half, we see a whole circle in the sky. It's a full moon!

Earth

sunlight

Some people like to track the moon during the lunar month. They enjoy watching the different phases. Do you know what phase the moon is in tonight?

This image shows the 28 phases of one lunar month. By adding these phases to a calendar, people can calculate the moon's phase for any date in the future.

Full Moon Effects

Some people believe that full moons affect how humans and animals act. Full moons are said to cause more intense emotions and bad behavior. Some people claim there are more crimes, traffic accidents, and visits to hospital emergency rooms during a full moon. Animals are thought to be more likely to bite people.

Most scientific studies, however, have disproved these theories. What do you think? Pay attention during the next full moon, and decide for yourself!

22

CHAPTER 3

A Different World

← The moon has more than 3 trillion craters.

The moon is close to Earth. However, if you went to the moon, you would find a very different world. The surface is covered with **craters**, or holes. The temperature is either burning hot or freezing cold. And there is no weather there at all!

The moon's surface looks lighter in places where it is higher.

The moon does not have significant **atmosphere**, or a blanket of gases surrounding it. Most planets have an atmosphere. If you went to the moon, you would not need your raincoat or umbrella. Without an atmosphere, there can't be rain, snow or wind! So there is no weather on the moon.

Earth's atmosphere soaks up heat and helps keep temperatures steady. On the moon, the sun can heat the surface to 265°F (129°C). That is hotter than boiling water!

The part of the moon that isn't facing the sun may have temperatures as low as −170°F (−112°C) or lower. That's about 50°F (28°C) colder than Antarctica, the coldest place on Earth.

The clouds around Earth show that Earth has an atmosphere. The moon never has clouds like Earth's.

Earth's atmosphere is all around you. It contains a gas called oxygen. Humans and animals need oxygen to survive. On the moon, there is no oxygen to breathe. So you would need to wear a space suit with a built-in supply of oxygen. Along with an oxygen supply, your space suit would also need its own heat and air-conditioning. This is because the lack of significant atmosphere on the moon causes extreme temperatures.

Astronauts practice walking in space suits on Earth before wearing them in space.

Here is an illustration of the surface of the moon. The sky is clear because the moon has no atmosphere.

Sound can't travel on the moon.

The moon is a quiet place—in fact, there is no sound at all! On Earth, when something makes a sound, **sound waves** travel through the atmosphere. When the sound waves reach your ears, you hear the sound. The moon has no atmosphere. Sound waves have nothing to travel through. This means you can't hear a thing!

Underwear

Under the suit, astronauts wear special space underwear with tubes of water running through it. The water keeps them cool. A cap under the helmet has a microphone and earphones so astronauts can talk to one another.

Layers

The suit is 11 layers thick and very strong. It weighs almost 300 pounds (136 kilograms).

Control Panel

With the push of a button, astronauts can control their temperature and air supply.

Gloves

Astronauts need to use small tools while wearing these thick gloves. To get the best fit, the gloves are custom made for each astronaut. They cost $40,000 a pair!

Safe in Space

It's always cold and dark in space. There is no air. Deadly rays from the sun, and fast-flying space rocks could do serious damage. But inside this $2 million space suit, you would feel fine!

Backpack

This pack holds the astronaut's air supply. It also has a fan to keep air moving inside the suit. And it holds batteries that keep its equipment running.

Visor

This visor is covered with a thin layer of pure gold. It protects astronauts from the sun's blinding rays.

Light from a full moon reflects off the sea along the coast of Australia.

CHAPTER 4

Moonscape

When there are two full moons in one month, the second one is called a "blue moon."

The moon has been the subject of songs and poems. People think that moonlight is romantic. If you were on the moon, you might think differently, however.

Rocky soil covers the surface of the moon.

The moon has been described as looking empty and strange. You would not find any green grass, blooming trees, or colorful flowers there. The moon is different shades of black, white, and gray.

There are also no oceans, rivers, or streams. There might be frozen water, however. The moon has a north pole and a south pole, just as Earth does. Some **astronomers** now think that frozen water may be trapped in craters near the moon's cold poles.

Most of the moon's surface is covered with a fine layer of dust. Astronauts left their footprints in this dust. Pictures of these footprints were sent back to Earth and seen around the world. Those footprints are still on the moon. There is no wind or flowing water to sweep them away!

The last astronaut to walk on the moon was Eugene Cernan. No humans have visited it since December 14, 1972.

Astronauts' footprints have been on the moon since 1969.

You would also find lots of rocks on the moon. Some rocks are as small as a grain of sand. Others are larger than houses! These rocks do not get worn down by wind or flowing water, as Earth's rocks do. They remain the same over time.

The darker smooth area in this photograph is called *Mare Imbrium*, which means the "Sea of Rains."

Mare Imbrium

Maria, Highlands, and Craters

The moon's surface has plains, mountains called highlands, and craters. When you look at the moon, do you see dark areas? These are plains called maria (MAR-ee-uh). *Maria* is the Latin word for "seas."

The maria formed long ago. At the time, there were active volcanoes on the moon. When these volcanoes erupted, lava flowed from them. Thick layers of lava hardened to form these smooth plains.

There are also bright areas on the moon. These are the mountains, or lunar highlands. The highlands are a light gray color and are higher than the maria.

The round circles you see when you look at the moon are its craters. Some craters are the remains of very old volcanoes. Other craters were made when zooming space rocks slammed into the moon.

Under the Moon's Surface

No one can see all the way to the moon's center. But astronauts have used equipment to take samples of rock from beneath the moon's surface. And astronomers have used what they know about Earth's structure to understand the moon.

Astronomers believe that the moon has four main layers. The outermost layer is a thin layer of rock called the **crust**. Under the crust is a thick layer of rock called the mantle. The center of the moon is called the **core**. It is made of two layers. Its outer layer is soft rock. Its innermost part is metal.

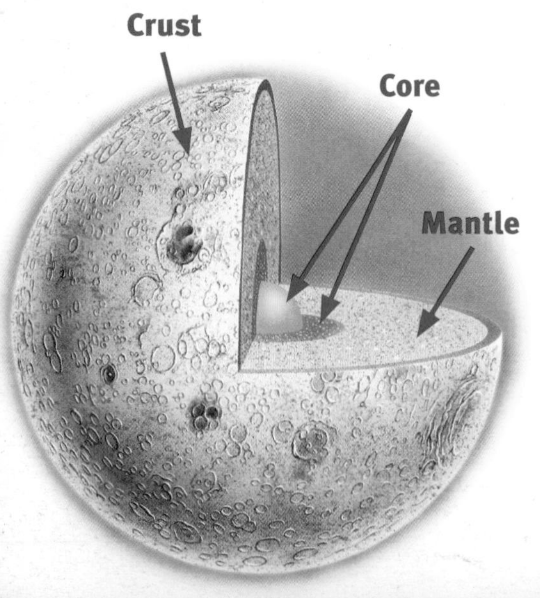

Crust

Core

Mantle

This diagram shows what the moon might look like if a section were cut out of it.

How Was the Moon Formed?

The moon may seem very different from Earth. Yet most astronomers believe that the moon came from Earth.

It all started about 4.5 billion years ago. That was when Earth and the rest of the solar system formed. Back then, Earth's rock was melted into a liquid.

Astronomers think that an object the size of

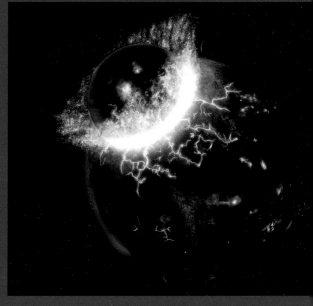

This illustration shows a large object hitting Earth. An impact like this could have formed the moon.

Mars struck the liquid Earth. Parts of Earth and the huge object were hurled into space. Gravity caused them to clump together to form Earth's moon.

This illustration shows a view of Earth from the moon.
Astronauts on the moon saw something similar to this.

CHAPTER 5

Going to the Moon

Twelve astronauts have walked on the moon.

Can you imagine leaving Earth to go to the moon? Astronauts have already done that. They blasted off and traveled through space at a speed of 25,000 miles (40,234 km) per hour. It took them three days to reach the moon.

Astronaut Alan Shepard planted the American flag on the moon in 1971.

39

In total, *Apollo* astronauts brought 842 pounds (382 kg) of moon rocks and dust back to Earth.

On July 20, 1969, Neil Armstrong became the first person to walk on the moon. He was one of the astronauts on the *Apollo 11* spacecraft.

Between July 1969 and December 1972, six *Apollo* spacecraft went to the moon. Astronauts collected rocks and soil and gathered information about the moon's surface.

During the 1990s, scientists sent spacecraft without astronauts to the moon. The instruments on board were controlled by computers on Earth.

The spacecraft *Clementine* was launched in 1994. The *Lunar Prospector* was launched in 1998. These spacecraft sent back pictures and other information that suggested there might be frozen water on the moon.

People have visited the moon. But will anyone ever *live* there? NASA (the National Aeronautics and Space Administration) has announced that it plans to build a base on the moon where people can live. Astronauts will travel to the moon by 2020 to begin this mission.

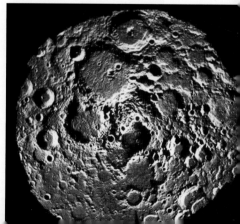

Images taken by *Clementine* were put together to create this view of the moon's north pole.

Once completed, the base will be a temporary home for astronauts and scientists. It will also be a science laboratory. It could even be a first stop on a trip to Mars!

Who knows what the future will bring? Today, you are reading this book on Earth. Someday, you could be visiting a library on the moon. After all, you will need something to read on your trip to outer space. ★

Here is an artist's view of what a moon base may look like.

42

True Statistics

Distance from Earth: About 238,855 mi. (384,400 km)

Diameter: 2,159 mi. (3,475 km)

Atmosphere: Not significant

Number of days to orbit Earth: 29.5

Number of craters: More than 3 trillion

Size range of craters: From the size of a quarter to the South Pole–Aitken Basin, which is 1,560 mi. (2,511 km) across

Highest point: 37,326 ft. (11,377 m) high

Lowest point: Up to 42,650 ft. (13,800 m) deep, in the South Pole–Aitken Basin

Surface area: 14,645,750 sq. mi. (37,932,330 sq km)

Did you find the truth?

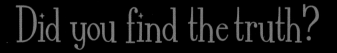

T There are footprints on the moon right now.

F Noises sound louder on the moon than they do on Earth.

Resources

Books

Birch, Robin. *The Moon*. Philadelphia: Chelsea Clubhouse, 2004.

Buckley, James. *Space Heroes: Amazing Astronauts*. New York: DK, 2004.

Chrismer, Melanie. *The Moon*. Danbury, CT: Children's Press, 2008.

Knudsen, Shannon. *Neil Armstrong*. Minneapolis: Lerner, 2003.

Kramer, Barbara. *Neil Armstrong: Meet the Famous Astronaut*. Berkeley Heights, NJ: Enslow Publishers, 2003.

Lassieur, Allison. *Astronauts*. Danbury, CT: Children's Press, 2000.

Miller, Heather. *Astronaut*. Chicago: Heinemann Library, 2003.

Mitchell, Melanie. *Moon*. Minneapolis: Lerner, 2004.

Tomecek, Steve. *Moon*. Washington, DC: National Geographic Society, 2004.

Organizations and Web Sites

The Apollo Program

www.nasm.si.edu/apollo

Get more information on the Apollo moon missions.

Lunar and Planetary Institute: Fun With Science—Colonies

www.lpi.usra.edu/education/explore/colonies

Check out this Web site to learn more about space colonies.

Young Astronaut Council

5200 27th Street W

Washington, DC 20015

301-617-0923

Join a program that promotes learning about science and math by studying space.

Places to Visit

Kennedy Space Center

Kennedy Space Center
FL 32899
321-867-5000
www.ksc.nasa.gov
Explore NASA's launch headquarters and learn more about some of the organization's space missions

Smithsonian National Air and Space Museum

Independence Avenue at 4th Street, SW
Washington, DC 20560
202-633-1000
www.nasm.si.edu
This museum has the world's largest collection of historic spacecraft.

Important Words

astronomers (uh-STRAW-nuh-murz) – scientists who study the planets, stars, and space

atmosphere (AT-mu-sfihr) – the blanket of gases that surrounds a planet or other object

core – the center of a planet or moon

craters – holes created when space objects crash into moons or other objects

crust – the outermost layer of a rocky planet or moon

equator – an imaginary line around the center of a moon or a planet, halfway between the north and south poles.

gravity – a force that pulls two objects together

mass – the amount of matter, or stuff, in an object

orbits – travels around an object such as a sun or planet

phases – the different shapes the moon appears to have during the lunar month

rotates – spins on an axis

solar system (SOH-lur SISS-tuhm) – a sun and all the objects that travel around it

sound waves – vibrations that can be heard

Index

About the Author

Award-winning author Elaine Landau has a bachelor's degree from New York University and a master's degree in library and information science from Pratt Institute.

She has written more than 300 non-fiction books for children and young adults. Although Ms. Landau often writes on science topics, she especially likes writing about planets and space.

She lives in Miami, Florida, with her husband and son. The trio can often be spotted at the Miami Museum of Science and Space Transit Planetarium. You can visit Elaine Landau at her Web site: www.elainelandau.com.